Basil Brush and a Dragon

For Daniel

PETER FIRMIN

Basil Brush and a Dragon

KAYE & WARD
and
SCHOLASTIC PUBLICATIONS

First published by
KAYE & WARD LIMITED
21 New Street, London EC2M 4NT
1971
Reprinted 1975

ISBN 0 7182 0325 9 (hardback)
ISBN 0 7182 0345 3 (paperback)

All enquiries and requests relevant to this title should be sent to the publisher, Kaye & Ward Ltd, 21 New Street, London EC2M 4NT, and not to the printer.

Printed in England by
TINLING (1973) LTD

Basil Brush is a clever fox.
He likes to read stories to Harry the mole.

Harry has many story-books.
He has books about animals and birds.

He has exciting books about space-travel.

He has books about pirates and witches and dragons and other exciting things.

Each day Harry would choose
a different story.
"Today," he said to Basil,
"I will choose a story about a king;
a king who was bold, in days of old,
and killed a fierce bad dragon."

So Basil told Harry the story about the king. It was about a fierce and fiery dragon who frightened all the people. The king put on his helmet and took his lance. He rode on his brave horse to kill the dragon.

Harry liked that story very much.

Basil and Harry went to bed.
Basil was tired and went to sleep.
Harry did not go to sleep at once.
"Basil," he said from his little bed.
Basil grunted.
"Basil," said Harry once again.
Basil snorted.
"May I ask you a question?" asked Harry.

"Tomorrow," grumbled Basil.
"May we go hunting for dragons?"
asked Harry.
"Tomorrow," mumbled Basil, as he dropped off to sleep again.
Harry was pleased.

Next morning Harry was very busy.
He was busy in the tool-shed.

He was busy in the village.
He was preparing for a dragon-hunt.

Basil and Harry had their lunch.
"It will be exciting," said Harry.
"Just like days of old,
when kings were bold,
and went to hunt the dragon."
"What are you babbling about, old bean?"
asked Basil.
"We are going to hunt a dragon today,"
said Harry. "You said we could."

"Did I say that?" said Basil. "How silly!
Well I don't think I can, not today."
"Surely you are not afraid?" said Harry.
Basil looked hurt.
"Of course I am not afraid," he said.
"If I had a lance I would hunt one.
I'd be off like a shot, as you know."

"Well, come on, then," said Harry.
He took Basil to the tool-shed.
"Here is your lance," he said.
He gave Basil a long bean-pole.

"Oh dear, how kind," said Basil.
"It's just what I needed, a lance.
With this lance I'd be bold,
like those kings of old,
but I haven't a helmet like them."

Harry went into the tool-shed.
"Here you are," he said. "Here is your helmet. Try it on."
The helmet was a cardboard box.
Harry tied it on with string.
Basil looked out of a slit in the side.

"I feel quite bold," said Basil. "With
a box on my head and a pole in my hand
I could go to hunt a dragon.
It's a pity that I have no horse."

Harry ran out of the garden.
Basil practised hunting dragons.

He swiped at the thistles.

He slashed at the grass.

He did feel quite bold.

"Your majesty," said Harry.
"The royal horse is ready."
Harry led Basil to the garden gate.

"That's a very odd looking horse," said Basil. "More like a dish-mop on legs. Are you sure that it isn't a dog?"

"Well yes, this is Alfred," said Harry.
"He is very good at hunting rabbits.
He probably hunts dragons too.
Shall we go?"

So the king rode out from his castle
on his brave horse.
His faithful servant ran on ahead
to find a dragon.

They stopped at the top of a hill.
"Look," said Harry. "Far across the meadow I see a fierce dragon, I see its shape against the sky."
"Forward! brave Alfred," called Basil.
"Forward to hunt the dragon!"
Alfred did not move.
"I think you say 'Rabbits'," said Harry.

"Rabbits!" cried Basil.
The brave horse wagged its tail, and ran.
The king rode over the meadow
to hunt the fierce dragon.

His brave horse carried him almost into the dragon's mouth. He plunged his lance deep into the dragon and fell off.

Alfred dug into the earth around the dragon's feet. The dragon fell to the ground.

"Oh, your majesty!" said Harry. "That was well done. It was brave and exciting and bold."

"It was nothing," said Basil.
"That dragon was not very fierce.
Let us go and find another."

The king sat on his brave horse.
His faithful servant looked around.
"Look!" said Harry. "Beyond the wood, behind the trees, I see a dragon moving."

"Forward! brave Alfred," Basil called.
"Forward to hunt the dragon!"
Alfred stood still.
"Don't forget to say 'Rabbits'," said Harry.
"Rabbits!" called Basil.

The king rode into the wood.
He rode through the trees to hunt
the fiery dragon.
The dragon stood on a wall
stamping its six legs in anger.
"Over, brave Alfred," cried Basil.

Alfred ran right up to the wall and then stopped. The king did not stop. He flew over the wall and plunged his lance into the dragon.
The dragon fell in a heap around the king and was still.
It was not fiery. It was wet.

From a house nearby came a shout.
"Is it a maiden in distress?" asked Harry.
"No, old chap," said Basil.
"It is a housewife in the kitchen.
Let us go somewhere else to find
a dragon."

The king rode back through the trees.
He rode up to the top of the hill.
His faithful servant looked around
but he did not see any dragons.
"I think the dragons have gone to sleep,"
said Harry. "It is getting late."

"Yes you are right," said Basil.
"See, my brave horse is thirsty.
His tongue is hanging out."
"Look," said Harry. "Your castle is near.
I will go and prepare a feast."

So the king rode back to his castle.
His faithful servant went ahead
to prepare a feast.

The king and his servant had their feast in the castle. They had soup and beans, and biscuits for the horse.

"Alfred must go now," said Harry. "It is getting dark. His master will be coming home from work."

"Goodbye, Alfred," said Basil. "I hope you will come hunting again."

Alfred wagged his tail as Harry took him to the door.

"Listen!" said Harry. "I hear a strange noise. I hear a grinding and a rumbling and a roaring. Can it be a dragon?"

Basil took up his lance. They all went outside to look for the dragon.
"There it goes!" said Harry.
The eyes of the dragon glowed in the dark.

Its dark shape lumbered over the field.
"Let us follow this dragon," said Basil.
"It is a very large dragon, so we will
wait until it goes to sleep."

The dragon stopped. It shut its eyes.
Alfred barked and ran towards it.
"Forward!" shouted Basil.

They ran shouting towards the sleeping dragon. They did not reach the dragon. They bumped into something else.

It was the farmer, returning from the field where he had left his combine. "Hullo!" he said. "What are you three up to?"

"We were going to fight the dragon," said Basil. "That wild dragon over there."

"That's no wild dragon," laughed the farmer.
"That one is tame, and it works for me.
It helps me to gather the harvest.
The only dragons I know are in the
story-books, and that's the best place
for them, if you ask me!"

Harry the mole has many story-books.
His favourite one is about a dragon.
"Look," he says. "There's a dragon in this story-book. And that's the best place for it if you ask me!"
Then he closes the book with a bang.

the end